Folens
AGES 9–11

✓Accessing...

HISTORY 5

D1796609

Rhona Whiteford

Acknowledgements

Ann Ronan Picture Library/Heritage-Images p.9a; Arthur WV Mace; Milepost 92 ½/CORBIS p. 28a; Bettmann/CORBIS pp. 4a, 13b, 26a, 29, 33, 37, 45; Chris Bland; Eye Ubiquitous/CORBIS p. 25b; Christie's Images/CORBIS p. 14a; COLUMBIA/MARVEL/THE KOBAL COLLECTION p. 32a; CORBIS p. 11; English Coal Mine from 'Cyclopaedia of Useful Arts & Manufactures', edited by Charles Tomlinson, c.1880s (engraving), Whymper, Josiah Wood (1813-1903)/Private Collection, Ken Welsh/www.bridgeman.co.uk p. 6; Dinner Time, from 'Sun Artists: A Serial of Artistic Photography', published 1889-91 (photo) by Frank Meadow Sutcliffe (1853-1941) Private Collection/www.bridgeman.co.uk p. 7; An Orange Seller, c.1865 (oil on canvas) by William McTaggart (1835-1910) Private Collection/www.bridgeman.co.uk p.9b; Lessons by Helen Allingham (1848-1926) Phillips, The International Fine Art Auctioneers, UK/www.bridgeman.co.uk p. 12a; Discovery of America by John and Sebastian Cabot, 1497, from 'Ballou's Pictorial Drawing-Room Companion', April 1855 (engraving) (b&w photo) by American School (19th century) Library of Congress, Washington D.C., USA/www.bridgeman.co.uk p. 43; Sir Walter Raleigh (1554-1618) trying to establish friendship with King Arromaia of Guiana, from 'Americae', engraved and written by Theodor de Bry (1528-98) (engraving) by Jacques Le Moyne (de Morgues) (d.1587/88) (after) Library of Congress, Washington D.C., USA/www.bridgeman.co.uk p. 44; David Reed/CORBIS p. 34; English Heritage, National Monuments Record/Heritage-Images pp. 16a, 21; Fine Art Photographic Library/CORBIS p.8a; Gianni Dagli Orti/CORBIS p. 39; Gillian Darley; Edifice/CORBIS p. 25a; HANNAH BARBERA PRODS/ATLAS ENTERTAINMENT/THE KOBAL COLLECTION p. 32b; Historical Picture Archive/CORBIS pp. 14b, 46; Hulton-Deutsch Collection/CORBIS pp. 5a, 12b, 13a, 18b, 20a, 20b, 26b, 27a, 27b, 28b, 31a, 31b, 36; Ian Harwood; Ecoscene/CORBIS p. 35; Joel W. Rogers/CORBIS p. 40; Mary Evans Picture Library pp. 10, 23; Michael S. Yamashita/CORBIS p. 30; Museum of London/Heritage-Images pp. 15, 18a; NRM, York/Heritage-Images p. 4b; Robert Harding World Imagery pp. 16b, 38, 48; Sean Sexton Collection/CORBIS p.8a; Stapleton Collection/CORBIS p. 5b; WildCountry/CORBIS p. 17

© 2005 Folens Limited, on behalf of the author.
United Kingdom: Folens Publishers, Apex Business Centre, Boscombe Road, Dunstable, LU5 4RL.
Email: folens@folens.com

Ireland: Folens Publishers, Greenhills Road, Tallaght, Dublin 24.
Email: info@folens.ie

Poland: JUKA, ul. Renesansowa 38, Warsaw 01-905.

Folens publications are protected by international copyright laws. All rights are reserved. The copyright of all materials in this publication, except where otherwise stated, remains the property of the publisher and author. No part of this publication may be reproduced, stored in a retrieval system, or transmitted, in any form or by any means, for whatever purpose, without the written permission of Folens Limited.

Rhona Whiteford hereby asserts her moral right to be identified as the author of this work in accordance with the Copyright, Designs and Patents Act 1988.

Commissioning editor: Zoë Nichols
Editor: Melody Ismail
Layout artist: Patricia Hollingsworth
Illustrations: Mike Lacey (SGA Illustration and Design)
Cover design: Philippa Jarvis
Cover image: Hulton-Deutsch Collection/CORBIS

First published 2005 by Folens Limited.

Every effort has been made to contact copyright holders of material used in this publication. If any copyright holder has been overlooked, we should be pleased to make any necessary arrangements.

British Library Cataloguing in Publication Data. A catalogue record for this publication is available from the British Library.

ISBN 1 84303 773 4

Contents

Queen Victoria

Paddington Station, 1862

© Folens

Victorian housing

The coal mine

© Folens

Winter ploughing

Coach and horses

Dockland and steam boats

© Folens

Brickworks

The orange seller

Wealthy Victorians

© Folens

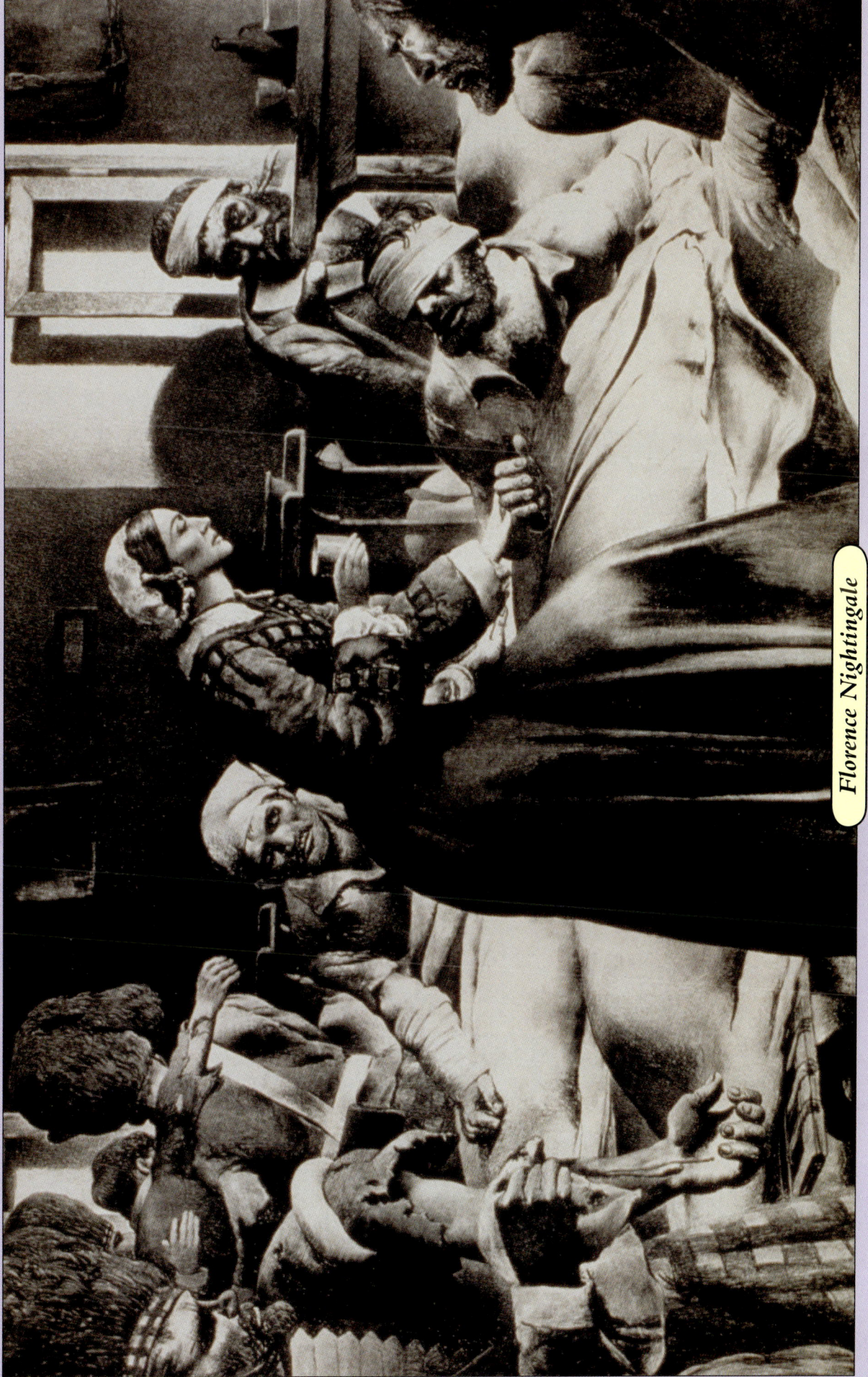

Florence Nightingale

Children and governess

A ragged school

© Folens

Victorian clothing

© Folens

Punch and Judy

Sea bathing

© Folens

Orphans

Victorian homes

© Folens

The Natural History Museum, built 1871

© Folens

Corner shop

Steam lifeboat

© Folens

Victorian farming

© Folens

Iron Bridge, Cornwall

St Pancras Station, London

© Folens

Blackpool promenade, 1894

A Victorian school

BOYS

GIRLS & INFANTS

© Folens

INLAND REVENUE.
LICENCE.—FOR ONE MALE SERVANT, 15s. 0d.
32 & 33 Vict., cap. 14.

No. _17_ _Revd W M Lui_

of _Ditcheat_ in the

Parish of _Ditcheat_ within the

Administrative County* _____ of _SOMERSET_

is hereby authorised to employ ONE MALE SERVANT from the day of
the date hereof until the 31st day of December next following; the sum of
FIFTEEN SHILLINGS having been paid for this Licence.

Granted at _CASTLE CARY:_

this _14_ day of _Jany_ 189_1_.

by _J E Bird_

NOTICE.

1. This Licence must be renewed at the expiration of this year, if you continue to keep a Servant.
2. Should an additional Servant be employed in the interval, a further Licence must be obtained.

*If the residence is within an Administrative County Borough insert "Borough".

A licence for a servant

Victorian artefacts

© Folens

London highrise flats

Radcliff Quay, Bristol

Schooling in the 1950s

© Folens

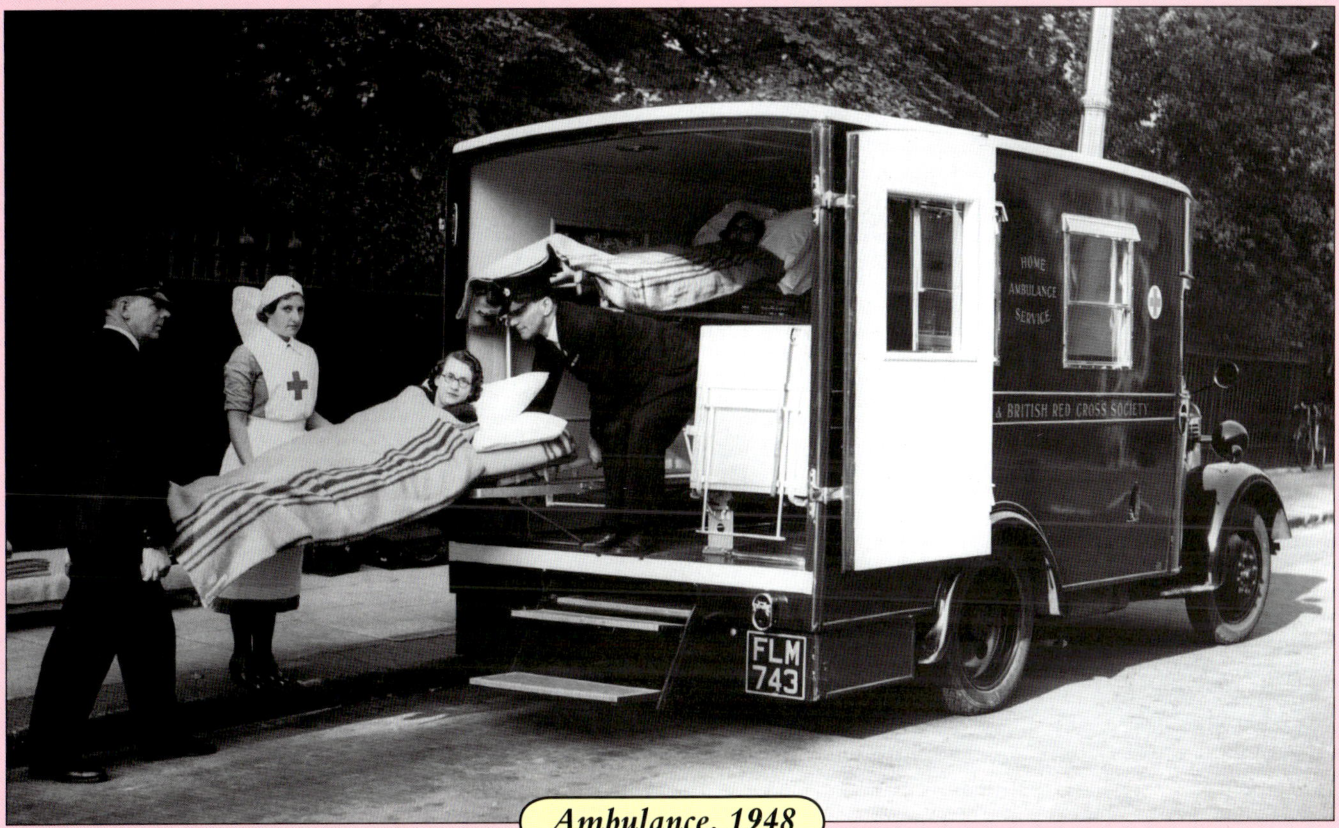

Ambulance, 1948

Air ambulance, present day

© Folens

The steam engine 'Burma'

The first turbine-driven airplane for fare-paying passengers, 1950

© Folens

Children of the 1950s

Tourists visit the Great Wall of China

© Folens

*Watching football,
London, 1949*

Girls playing, Liverpool, 1949

© Folens

Spiderman

Scooby Doo

© Folens

Buzz Aldrin walking on the Moon, 1969

© Folens

Battery hens

© Folens

Pollution on a UK beach

© Folens

A miner at the coalface

© Folens

A 'superstore', 1959

Buddhist temple, London

 © Folens

The Martellus map of the World

A replica of 'The Golden Hinde'

© Folens

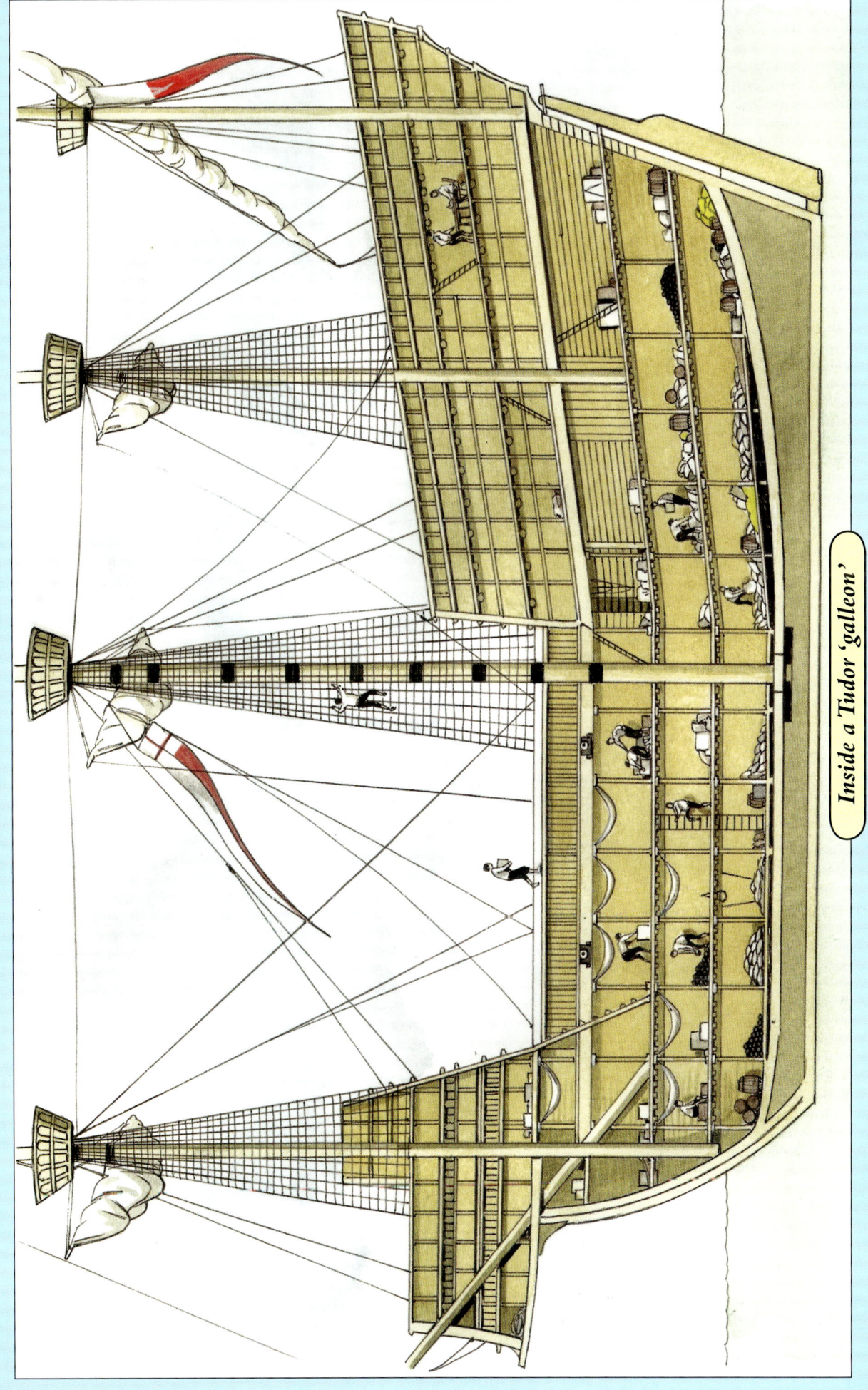

Inside a Tudor 'galleon'

Loading a Tudor ship

© Folens

John Cabot landing in Newfoundland

© Folens

Sir Walter Raleigh in Guiana

© Folens

Sir Francis Drake meeting a foreign prince

Christopher Columbus landing in the 'New World'

© Folens

Sir Walter Raleigh landing in Roanoke

Navajo tribe in ceremonial costume

© Folens